Weather Watch!

THE WEATHER
IN
SUMMER

Miriam Moss

Wayland

Weather Watch!

Other titles in this series include:
The Weather in Spring
The Weather in Autumn
The Weather in Winter

Cover pictures: Images of summer: (main picture) A single summer sunflower. (top left) Sunbathers on Kardamena Beach in Kos, Greece. (centre) A peacock butterfly. (bottom right) The midnight sun in Norway.

Contents page: Have you ever seen a lightning storm in summer? It is an exciting and dramatic sight. This storm is in California, USA.

Editor: Deb Elliott
Designer: Malcolm Walker

Text is based on *Summer Weather* in the *Seasonal Weather* series published in 1990.

First published in 1994 by
Wayland (Publishers) Ltd
61 Western Road, Hove
Sussex, BN3 1JD, England

© Copyright Wayland (Publishers) Ltd

British Library Cataloguing in Publication Data
Moss, Miriam
 Weather in Summer. - (Weather Watch! Series)
 I. Title II. Series
 551.6

ISBN 0-7502-1183-0
Typeset by Kudos
Printed and bound by Casterman S.A., Belgium

CONTENTS

ALL SORTS OF SUMMERS!

Look at this map. Can you find the tropics, the band of countries in the middle of the world? It is always warm here. Right on the equator, it is always hot and there are heavy, warm rains all the year round. ➡

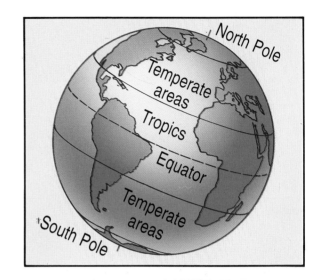

↓ Summer to some people means splashing about in the warm sea.

← *This beach is in Barbados, a hot, tropical island where the weather is always warm.*

Where is there thick snow and ice on the ground in summer? Where do giant icebergs stay frozen all the year round? Where does the Sun shine all day and all night in summer? At the North and South Poles! →

We live on Earth, a planet which spins round the Sun. The Sun shines on half the Earth at a time. The half that is lit by the Sun has daytime. The half that is in darkness has night. ➡

⬇ The Earth tilts as it spins round the Sun. The part that tilts towards the Sun has summer.

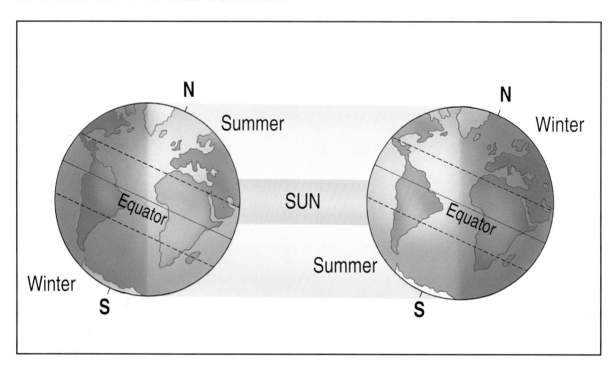

↑ *When the Sun rises early in the morning it floods our world with light. Here, the Sun rises at Stonehenge in England on Midsummer's Day.*

The longest day in northern temperate countries is the 21 June. It is called Midsummer's Day, even though it is near the beginning of summer.

In between the North and South Poles and the tropics are temperate countries. They have four clear changes in the weather each year. These are called seasons.

HOTTER AND HOTTER!

Look at the diagram opposite. Can you see that the rays from the Sun don't have to travel so far to reach the tropics?
This means that the Sun's rays are much stronger there than at the North and South Poles.

Can you see where the sunshine is weakest on the diagram? ➡

⬇ In summer the Sun shines all through the night in northern Norway!

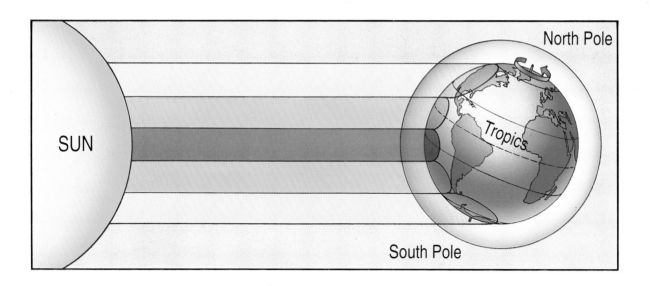

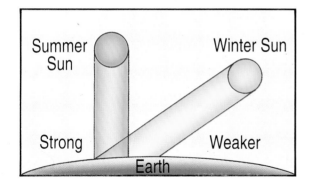

⬆ *Summer is warmer than winter because the Sun's rays are stronger and there are more hours of daylight.*

Did you know?

The hottest temperature recorded in Africa is 58°C (136.4°F).

The hottest temperature at the South Pole is only 14°C (57.2°F).

SUMMER WINDS

When the wind blows sometimes we feel a gentle breeze on our faces. At other times the wind blows so hard it nearly bowls us over. Winds can be cold and warm. Did you know that warm air is lighter than cool air? So warm air rises and cool air sinks.

We can't see the air pressing down all around us. A lot of cool air pressing down on us is heavier than a lot of warm air. We call this high pressure. The wind blows when air moves from where there is high pressure to where there is low pressure.

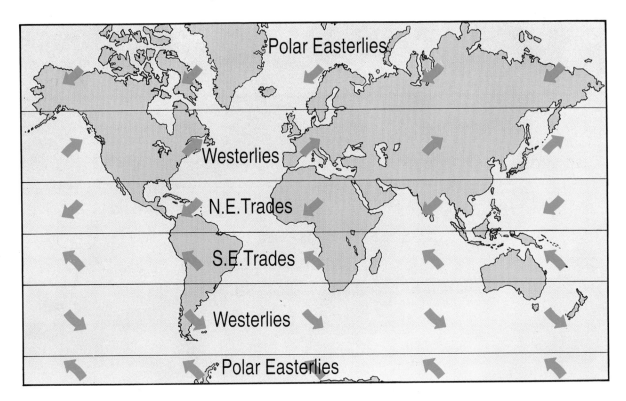

Polar Easterlies

Westerlies

N.E.Trades

S.E.Trades

Westerlies

Polar Easterlies

↑ *This map shows which way the main winds usually blow.*

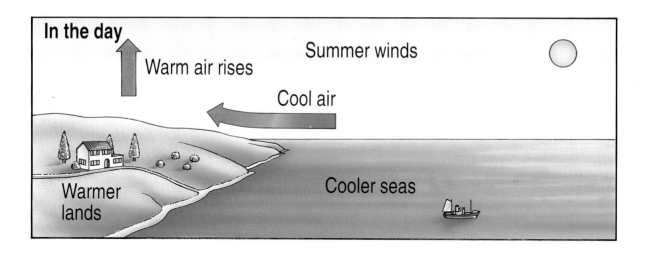

In the day

Summer winds

Warm air rises

Cool air

Warmer lands

Cooler seas

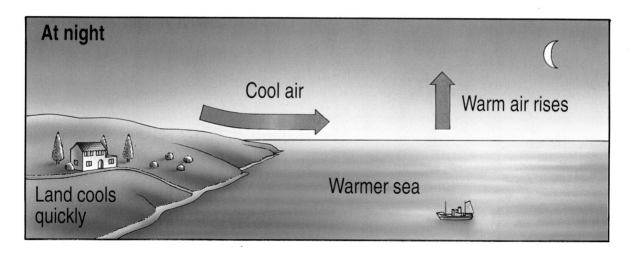

At night

Cool air

Warm air rises

Land cools quickly

Warmer sea

↑ *Look at the two diagrams above. In the daytime the cool air over the sea is sucked on to the land. At night, when the Sun sets, the land cools more quickly than the sea. The cooler air over the land is sucked out over the sea.*

SUDDEN SHOWERS

Sudden showers in summer can take you by surprise! ➡

⬇ *The three diagrams below show you when clouds can form.*

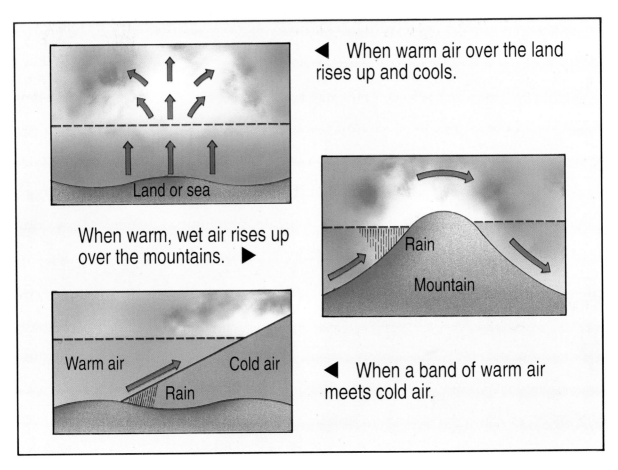

◀ When warm air over the land rises up and cools.

Land or sea

When warm, wet air rises up over the mountains. ▶

Rain

Mountain

Warm air   Cold air

Rain

◀ When a band of warm air meets cold air.

↑ *A field of sweet corn wrecked by a fierce summer hailstorm.*

When the tiny water droplets in clouds join together and get too heavy, they fall as rain. If raindrops freeze they become hailstones. Hailstones can become so heavy that they fall to the ground.

MONSOONS

In tropical countries monsoon winds bring giant thunderstorms. Thick rain clouds darken the sky. The air is hot, steamy and uncomfortable. Heavy rain splatters down on to the rooftops. Sometimes huge amounts of rainwater flood the street and wash away houses.

↓ *Look how dark monsoon clouds have gathered over the coast of Sri Lanka.*

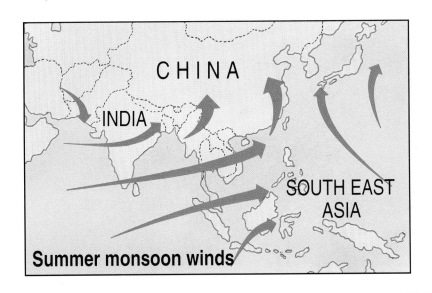

CHINA

INDIA

SOUTH EAST ASIA

Summer monsoon winds

↑ *From the map we see how, in summer, fierce monsoon winds blow in off the cool sea towards the hot air over Asia. Sometimes the monsoon rains don't arrive. Then the crops can't grow and there is not enough food for everyone.*

Monsoon rains have flooded this street in Calcutta, India. ➡

Summer thunderstorms can be spectacular. Loud rolls of thunder follow great flashes of lightning - and the rain pours down. Do you know why this happens?

In summer, warm, wet air rises up and cools to make thunderclouds. Electricity builds up in the thunderclouds until giant sparks break out. This is the lightning.

A lightning flash heats the air it passes through to 30,000°C (about 54,000°F)! No wonder the air booms with shock!

← *Lightning is really a giant spark of electricity.*

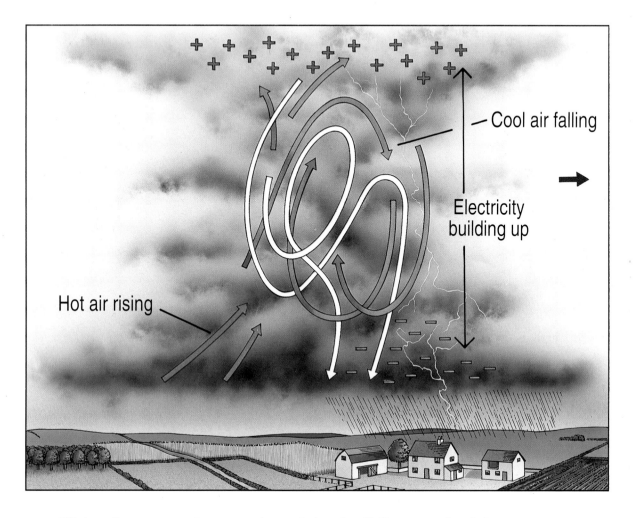

Cool air falling

Electricity building up

Hot air rising

↑ *This diagram shows electricity building up inside a thundercloud.*

The lightning flash makes the air it passes through very, very hot. This causes a shock wave - which is the thunder. It sounds just like the boom of a supersonic aircraft.

17

SUCKING AND SPOUTING

In summer thunderclouds gather and violent storms follow. In the USA tornadoes sometimes form at the bottom of the thundercloud.

A tornado is a whirling funnel of air that reaches down to the ground and sucks things up. It is just like a giant vacuum cleaner! There are different kinds of tornadoes. Some twitch and snake about like a hosepipe.

↑ *Tornadoes whirl around at up to 500 kilometres per hour.*

← *Strong tornadoes are dangerous. They suck up trees and tear the roofs off houses.*

Waterspouts move across the sea throwing spray into the air. →

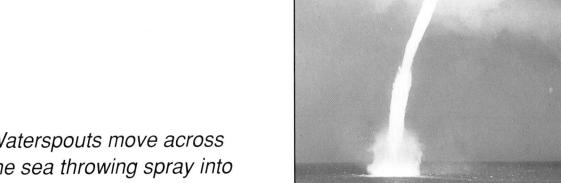

SUMMER SEASONS

There are many different summers all over the world. Near the North Pole the ice in the top few centimetres of soil melts in summer. This allows mosses and flowers to grow. The earth further underground stays frozen which means trees cannot grow here.

↓ *Some flowering shrubs grow in Alaska in summer. However, temperatures rarely rise above 10 °C (50 °F).*

↑ *Summer in temperate countries is not always sunny. Look at these dark summer storm clouds hanging over this French town.*

Many parts of the world have long hours of sunshine in the summer. ➡

STEAMY TROPICS

Countries which lie on the equator have hot weather all year round. They also have very heavy rains. This makes them perfect places for rainforests to grow. ➡

⬇ Mount Kilimanjaro, Africa's highest mountain, is so high it still has snow on top even in the summer!

↑ *At the edge of the rainforests where there is less rain, there are flat grasslands with a few trees.*

The photograph above shows the grasslands in Africa where the famous wild animals roam in the hot Sun looking for water holes.

DESERT SUMMERS

Camels drinking from a
waterhole in a cold Asian
desert. ➡

⬇ In hot desert lands the
weather is always hot and dry.
Rain hardly ever falls. There
are endless kilometres of
sand dunes where only wild
grasses grow. Cold deserts
have cool summers and
cold winters.

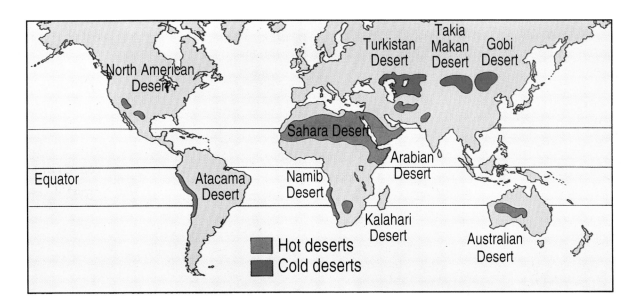

↑ *The world's hot and cold deserts.*

The hot Sahara Desert usually has more than ten hours of sunshine a day. The temperature can read 87°C (189°F). In cold deserts, like the Gobi, the summer temperature only reaches about 15°C (59°F)!

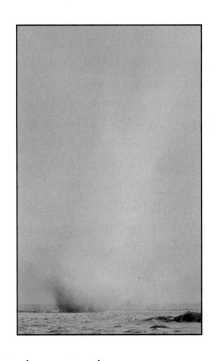

↑ *In hot deserts there are strong winds which whirl sand about, called dust devils.*

The Earth is slowly getting hotter and hotter. Gases from cars and factory chimneys trap the heat from the Sun. This means that less heat is escaping back into space. The world is heating up like a huge greenhouse. ➡

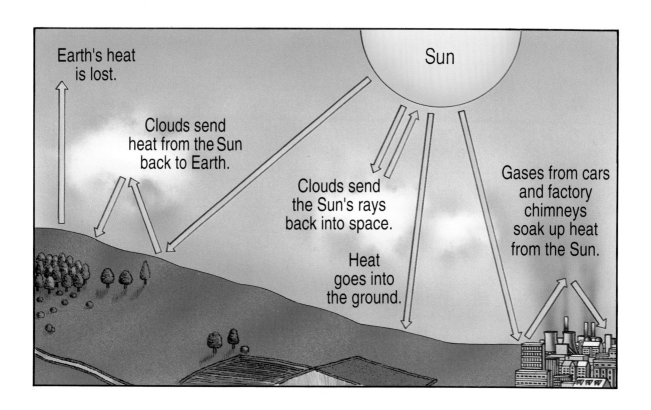

Earth's heat is lost.

Sun

Clouds send heat from the Sun back to Earth.

Clouds send the Sun's rays back into space.

Gases from cars and factory chimneys soak up heat from the Sun.

Heat goes into the ground.

↑ *Rainforests help to soak up damaging gases. Yet thousands of the valuable trees are cut down every day for wood or for grazing land.*

If we don't stop the world from heating up then more and more places will turn into deserts where food cannot grow. In time the ice at the North and South Poles will melt and cause terrible flooding. Many people are working hard to try and find ways of sorting out these problems.

CLOUD WATCH!

You can tell what the weather will be like by watching the clouds. If clouds move slowly when it is sunny, the sunny weather will stay. If they begin to move faster - watch out for wind and rain!

If the clouds which are higher up are moving in the same direction as the lower clouds, then the wind will change!

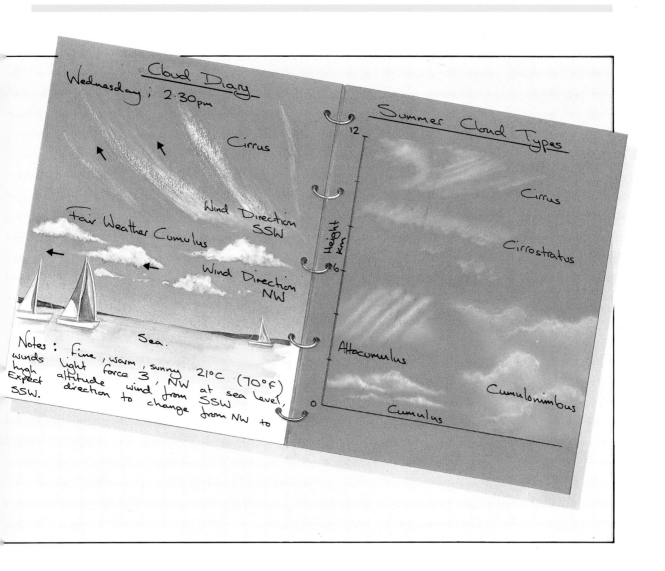

Keep a cloud diary for each day. Write down which way the clouds are moving and draw their shapes.

GLOSSARY

breeze A gentle, light wind.

desert A large area of very dry land.

equator An imaginary circle dividing the Earth into two equal parts.

flood A large amount of water covering normally dry land, often caused by heavy rain.

greenhouse A glass house which traps heat from the Sun.

hailstones Frozen raindrops.

iceberg A huge block of ice floating in the sea.

monsoon A wind in tropical countries that changes direction with the seasons. It often brings heavy rainstorms.

pressure When something presses down on us we feel pressure.

rainforest A thick forest found in tropical countries which have heavy rainfall.

spark A flash of light made by electricity.

supersonic Something which travels faster than sound travels.

temperature The amount of hotness in something.

tilt Leaning over to one side.

Books to read

Let's Celebrate Summer by Rhoda Nottridge (Wayland, 1994)

Projects for Summer by Celia McInnes (Wayland, 1988)

Summer Festivals by Mike Rosen (Wayland, 1990)

Sunny Weather by Jillian Powell (Wayland, 1992)

Weather and its Work by David Lambert and Ralph Hardy (Orbis, 1988)

Windy Weather by Jillian Powell (Wayland, 1992)

Picture acknowledgements
Bryan and Cherry Alexander 5 (right); Bruce Coleman Ltd cover, bottom right (Dr Eckart Pott), 8 (Dr Eckart Pott), 14 (Dieter and Mary Plage), 15 (D. Houston), 18 (W, Carlson/Lane), 25 (Leonard Lee Rue), 27 (Dieter and Mary Plage); Frank Lane Picture Agency 13, 19 (both), 20, 22 (both); Hutchison Library 21 (top), 23, 24 (top); J. Allan Cash 12; Meterological Office (r.K. Pilsbury), 28; Tony Stone Worldwide cover, main picture (Oliver Benn), top left (Chris Haigh), centre (Mervyn Rees), contents page, 7, 16, 21 (bottom), 24 (bottom); Wayland Picture Library 4 (Chris Fairclough), 26; Zefa Picture Library 5 (left), 6. All artwork is by the Hayward Art Group, except page 6 which is by Peter Bull.

INDEX